BRACE~~~~~~~~~~~~~~~~~~~~~~~~~~~~~~~~SCHOOL

BRACEVILLE, ILLINOIS

FIRST GRADE

	DATE DUE		
out ~~2~~	~~MAY 19 70~~ (2)		
~~2~~ ~~9~~			
~~9 29~~			
~~FEB 2 5 1988~~			
~~NOV~~			
~~4/7/04~~			
~~12-6-08~~ (2)			
~~11-14-08~~ (R)			
~~12-3-08~~ (R)			
~~MAR 25 '12~~ (1)			

Chandoha, Walter

A Foal for you.

A
FOAL
FOR YOU

With words and photographs by

WALTER CHANDOHA

A *Holly* BOOK

THE WORLD PUBLISHING COMPANY

CLEVELAND AND NEW YORK

Published by The World Publishing Company, 2231 West 110th Street, Cleveland, Ohio 44102. Published simultaneously in Canada by Nelson, Foster & Scott Ltd. First Printing 1967. Copyright © 1967 by Walter Chandoha. All rights reserved. No part of this book may be reproduced in any form without written permission from the publisher, except for brief passages included in a review appearing in a newspaper or magazine. Library of Congress Catalog Card Number: 67–15216. Printed in the United States of America.

Here is a foal for you—a baby horse, just born.
Her mother stays very near.

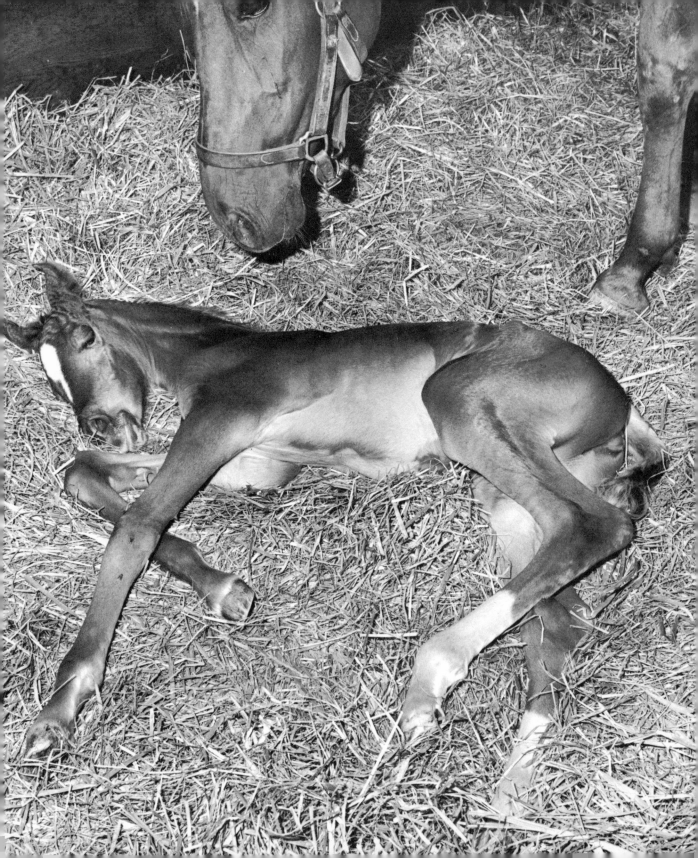

It is not easy for the foal to stand up at first.

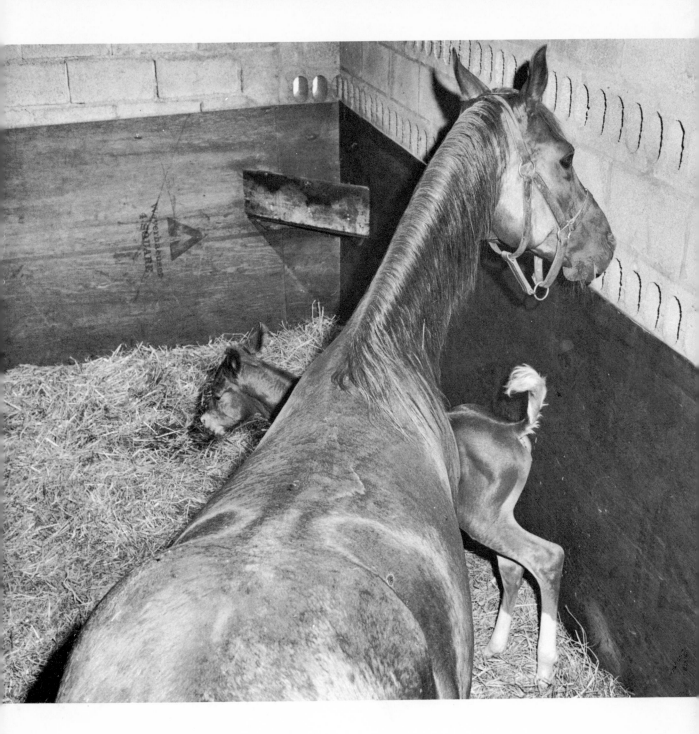

Then she wobbles to her very first meal.
She likes the stable, with her mother there.

She has to be carried outdoors.

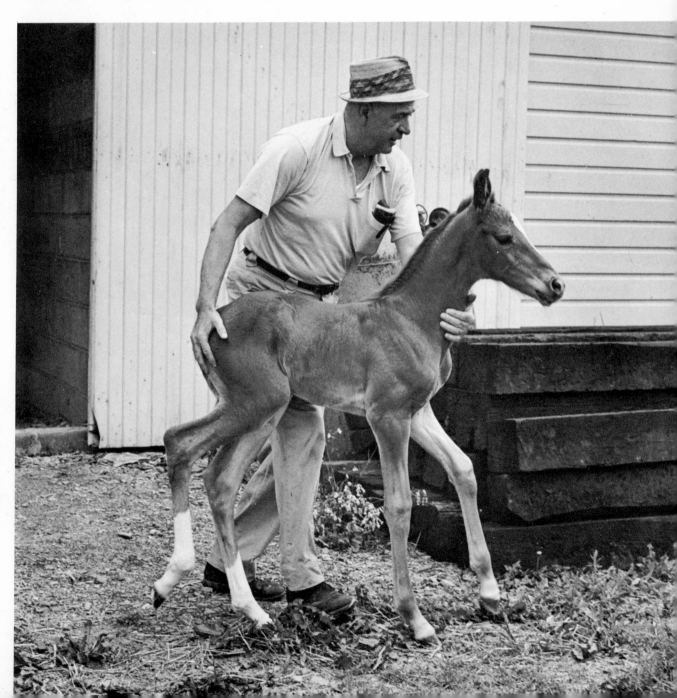

But here's her mother.
Now she's really safe.

She gallops a bit, but oh,

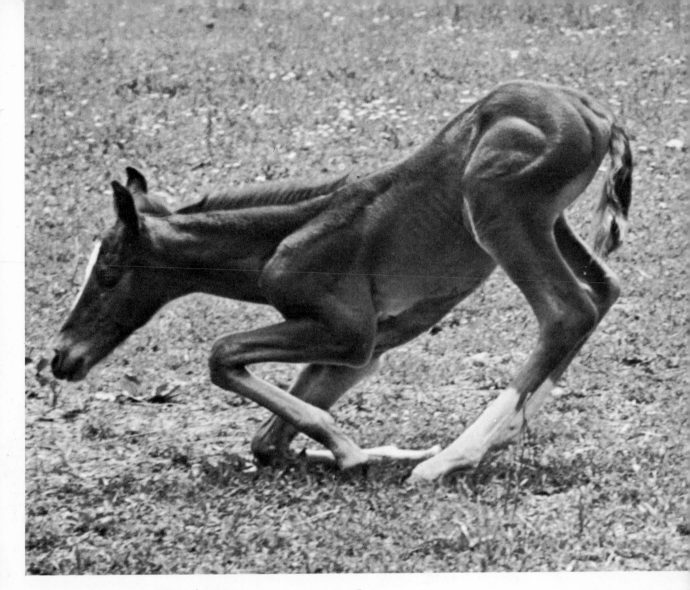

a bit too fast. Her legs are so very long.

She has to bend her knees to eat the grass.

Isn't that
a funny thing?

Now she is getting tired, and she needs a rest.

It is hard for her to get up again, but she will.

She runs around her mother

and then comes back again.

Sometimes she is having her regular meal, and sometimes

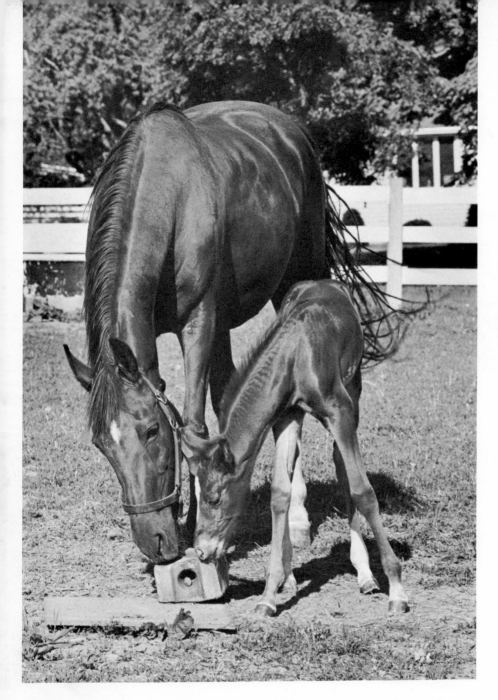

she licks a salt block, just like her mother does.
Salt is good for horses.

But see her now!

How she gallops and prances!

Now people begin to play with her,

and she is growing up.

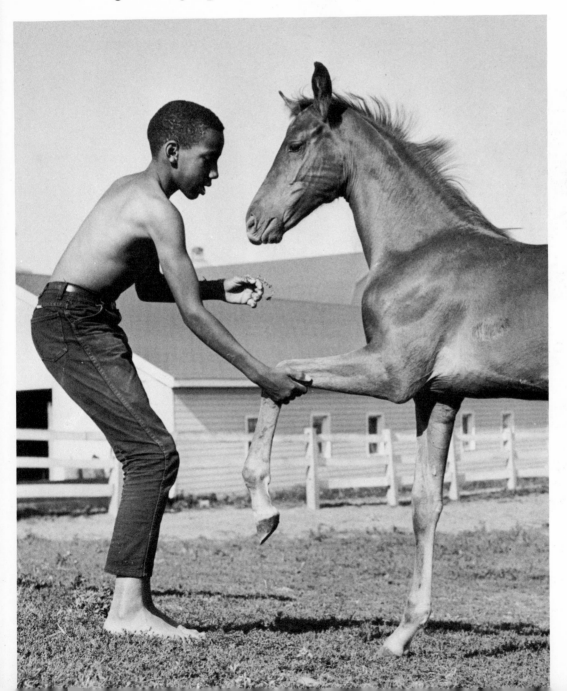

But she'll come back and be with you,
whenever you are ready.